The
Official Movie
Scrapbook

Because
of Winn
Dixie

Jean K. Kwon
photographs by
Suzanne Tenner

CANDLEWICK PRESS
CAMBRIDGE, MASSACHUSETTS

Contents

Hi there! My name is **Winn-Dixie**. It's a funny name, I know—but that's what Opal called me when she first saw me. As soon as I heard her call me by that name, I knew everything in my life had changed.

I was somebody. I was someone's dog. I was found.

Let me tell you how it all happened. Then I'll show you around town and introduce you to all my new friends and favorite places. Come on!

It all started when I wandered into a supermarket—
I'd never been inside one before, so I was curious.
As I was trotting through the aisles, sniffing around,
a big man with a furry lip saw me. He started to yell.
Then he began to chase me.

Hooray! I thought. *He wants to play tag!* I ran as fast
as I could. I darted left and right. I jumped over fruit
stands and ducked between people's legs. Other people
joined in. I wish you could've been there—it was a lot
of fun!

Here I am making a dash for it through the flower stand.

Finally, I tagged the furry-lipped man. I don't think
he liked to lose, because he began to cry. Just then,
I heard a voice—"Here, boy! Come on, boy! Come
on . . . Winn-Dixie!"—and just like that, I got a name.

Opal is my hero. She's also my best friend.

She took me home.

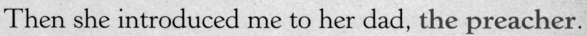

Then she introduced me to her dad, **the preacher**.

The preacher didn't seem too happy with the way I looked or smelled. I guess I was a bit of a mess.

Don't look! I'm taking a bath.

Ten Things I Know

1

She is likable—and lick-able!

2 She is a good writer.

About Opal

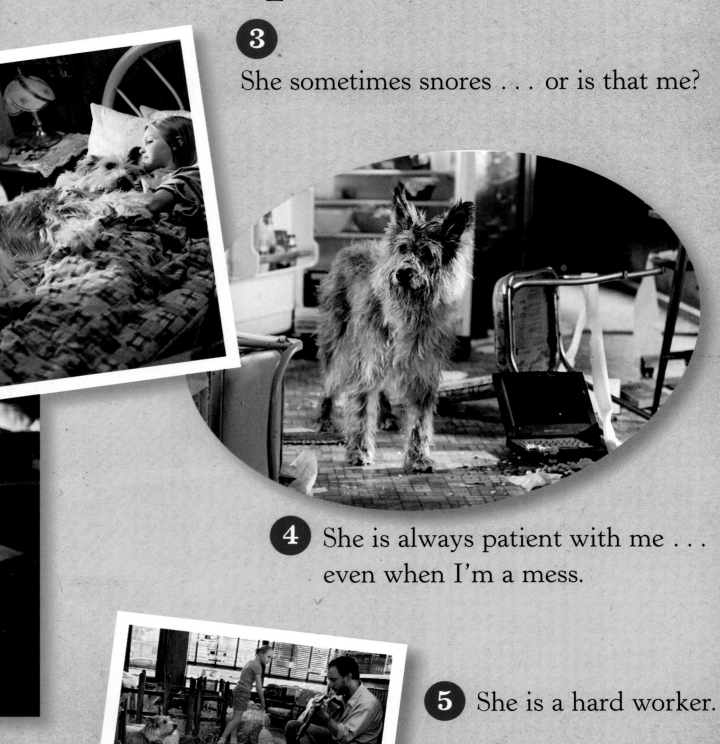

3 She sometimes snores . . . or is that me?

4 She is always patient with me . . . even when I'm a mess.

5 She is a hard worker.

She's good at making friends.

She loves parties—
and bringing
people together.

8 She looks out for me—even in the middle of thunderstorms.

9

She loves the preacher.

10 She loves me.

19

This is the Open Arms
Baptist Church, where
the preacher leads us all
in singing, praying, and
catching mice.

(Actually, I'm the only one
who does the mouse-catching.)

These are the Dewberry brothers: Dunlap and Stevie. They don't have much fur on their heads.

Amanda Wilkinson always looks like she's smelling something bad. She must have a better nose than I do.

I like **Sweetie Pie Thomas**. She gives me big hugs—though they can be a little wet at times, since she sucks on her front paw a lot.

Signs on wall: Mr. Alfred / Manager

Sign on railing: NO CHILDREN OR PETS ALLOWED

Mr. Alfred lives next door to us. Even though we all live in the Friendly Corners Trailer Park, he doesn't look too friendly, does he?

Actually, Mr. Alfred isn't so bad,
once you get to know him.

Opal and I go to Gertrude's Pets every day. She sweeps the floor and dusts the shelves while I hang out with my furry and feathered friends.

Gertrude likes to sit on my head and shout, "Dog!" I don't know why she thinks she has to remind me.

And this is **Otis**. He's a bit shy—but boy, can he play some beautiful music!

We all love to sit and listen.

The Herman W. Block Memorial Library is a great place to find books—and listen to stories.

When **Miss Franny Block** first saw me, she thought I was a grizzly bear. Can you imagine—me, a bear?

Opal and I like to listen to Miss Franny Block tell her stories, especially the ones about her great-grandfather Littmus Block. Sometimes she even gives us some of her **Littmus Lozenges**. They taste sweet, but they also taste *sad* somehow. They get me to thinking back on the time when I lived alone and didn't have Opal or my other friends.

The preacher taught me and Opal another word for sadness: *melancholy*. Melancholy is exactly what those Littmus Lozenges taste like.

This is our friend **Gloria Dump**. Gloria makes the best peanut-butter sandwiches I've ever eaten!

This is Gloria Dump's bottle tree. She says she hung all those bottles to keep away the ghosts of all the things she's done wrong.

Gloria sure has had some sorrows in her life. But things started to change for the better when she and Opal and I became friends.

Gloria even helped Opal plant a new type of tree—a wait-and-see tree. We're still waiting to see what kind of tree it will become.

With all the new friends Opal and I made, we threw ourselves a party in Gloria Dump's backyard. Here's who we invited:

Guest List

The Preacher

Gloria Dump

Miss Franny Block

Otis & Gertrude

Sweetie Pie Thomas

Amanda Wilkinson

Stevie Dewberry

Dunlap Dewberry

Mr. Alfred

Everybody made it
and had a fun time!

Gloria Dump made her famous Dump Punch and helped Opal make egg-salad sandwiches.

I couldn't help myself—I ate a few sandwiches before the guests arrived!

Otis brought Gertrude, his guitar, and some pickles.

Sweetie Pie brought pictures of dogs. Miss Franny had Littmus Lozenges for everyone.

A sudden thunderstorm crashed our party.
I'm terrified of thunderstorms. So I took off.

Opal and the preacher went looking
for me—right in the middle of all
that rain and thunder and lightning.

Ten Things I Know About Winn-Dixie

1. He has a pathological fear of thunderstorms.

2. He likes to smile, using all his teeth.

3. He can run fast.

4. He snores.

5. He can catch mice without squishing them to death.

6. He likes to meet people.

7. He likes to eat peanut butter.

8. He can't stand to be left alone.

9. He likes to sit on couches and sleep in beds.

10. He doesn't mind going to church.

—India Opal Buloni

Opal looked all over town for me—but I was hiding inside the house the whole time. In the end, she found me.

Throw Your Own *Becaus*

Follow these steps and throw your own party!

1 ## The Guest List

Make a list of all the people you'd like to invite. If your party is going to be pet friendly, don't forget to invite your favorite furry and feathered friends.

2 ## Invitations

Be creative and make your own invitations. Don't forget to include all the important information about the party.

You're invited to a PARTY!
date: Tomorrow
time: 2pm
place: Gloria Dump's Backyard
what to bring: Pickles, Littmus Lozenges
RSVP

Instead of mailing your invitations, why not hand-deliver them? It's a nice personal touch

f *Winn-Dixie* Party!

3 **Decorations**

Take Sweetie Pie's lead and decorate with pictures of dogs or other favorite pets.

4 **Refreshments**

Follow the recipes on the next pages to make your own Dump Punch and egg-salad sandwiches—and don't forget the peanut-butter dog treats for your four-legged guests!

Recipes

Winn-Dixie's Peanut-Butter Doggie Treats

1 ½ cups water

½ cup vegetable oil

2 eggs

3 tblsp. peanut butter

2 tsp. vanilla

2 cups flour

½ cup cornmeal

½ cup oats

Preheat oven to 400° F. Mix the water, oil, eggs, peanut butter, and vanilla together. In a separate bowl, whisk the flour, cornmeal, and oats together, then stir them into the wet mixture to form a ball. Roll out the dough to a ¼-inch thickness. Cut out dog treats in dog-bone or other shapes. Bake on a greased or nonstick cookie sheet for 20 minutes. Allow the treats to cool in the turned-off oven for about an hour. Store them in an airtight container. Makes one or two dozen treats. For dogs only!

Opal's Outstanding Egg-Salad Sandwiches

6 hard-boiled eggs
2 celery stalks
½ onion
½ cup mayonnaise

¼ tsp. salt
1 tomato (sliced)
4 lettuce leaves
8 slices of bread
frilly-topped toothpicks

Coarsely chop the eggs, celery, and onion. Place in a bowl, and mix in the mayonnaise and salt. Spread approximately 1 tablespoon of egg salad on each of 4 slices of bread. Top each with tomato slices, a lettuce leaf, and a slice of bread. Trim off the bread crusts, and cut each sandwich on both diagonals to create 4 small triangles. Skewer each triangle with a frilly-topped toothpick. Serves 4.

Gloria's Famous Dump Punch

orange juice
grapefruit juice
club soda, seltzer, or ginger ale

Mix equal parts of the orange juice, grapefruit juice, and soda in a large punch bowl. Serve chilled.

Behind the Scenes

Here's a look at the making of *Because of Winn-Dixie*.

The movie's director, Wayne Wang, wanted to find a dog that looked like the one on the cover of the original book. The delightful "star" he discovered is a Picardy shepherd, one of the oldest breeds of sheep-herding dogs, which orginally came from the Picardie region of France.

Director Wayne Wang gets kissed by Winn-Dixie.

When can I take this mouse out of my mouth?

Wayne Wang sets up the supermarket scene for AnnaSophia Robb (Opal).

Chatting with Elle Fanning
(Sweetie Pie)

Giving direction to
Dave Matthews (Otis)

Gloria's backyard is decorated for the party.

Searching for
Winn-Dixie in the
thunderstorm

Winn-Dixie and the book's
author, Kate DiCamillo